Poetry of a Life

SHARON ROMERO

ISBN: 979-8-9891452-4-9 (Paperback)
        979-8-9891452-5-6 (Ebook)

Olympus Story House

Contents

Why You and Me?

We fell in love on a summer day.
It was not long before I asked you to stay.
Why you and me?
It was you who gave me pain.
Then my tears fell like rain.
Why you and me?
It was you that gave me a son.
He was the only one.
Why you and me?
Now, we have had many years.
Our bodies have grown tired, and feelings are seldom desired.
Why you and me?
Often, we have been angered, and
things never seem to come together quite the same.
Why you and me?
Often, we disagree and never understand each other.
Why you and me?
Now, we have a granddaughter, and I still cannot help but wonder.
Why you and me?
Perhaps, one day, I will be set free of this question.
Why you and me?
Yet, even with my many sorrows, you have promised all your tomorrows.
So maybe that's my answer to
"Why you and me?"
For your love is strong, and you don't even contemplate it.
Why you and me?
As if you always knew what was meant to be.

1

Women without Notice

We work and clean without respect.
Just to have things dirty again within only thirty seconds.
Anger fills our hearts after a long day on the same dull task.
Our work seems so trivial and unimportant.
They ask "What is wrong, honey?"
As if they do not know.
When we are treated as if we live below.
We are women without notice.
All we get is "When is dinner?"
Or "Did you wash my clothes?"
Maybe "Have you seen my belt?"
We look so pretty without even being noticed.
We strive to look our best each day.
Yet, we are women without notice.
For our families, we fight the good fight.
We do our best to make everyone happy.
Yet, we are women without notice.
We turn a certain age and love just goes away.
We are women without notice.
At our age, they may call us cougars if we seek a younger gent after our
exhausting fight.
Yet, we are women without notice.
We hope for a hug, wink, or even some scuffle over us because after all . . .
We are women without notice.
Sadness fills us with tears at times because we know . . .
We are just women without notice.

If we could break away from these chains that keep us so muffled,
Only then will our freedom reveal that we stand out and no longer find
ourselves as women without notice.

You and I

You are my fire; I am your heat.
You are my love; I am your desire.
You are my sound; I am your quiet.
You are my strength; I am your comfort.
You are my laughter; I am your glow.
You are my sun; I am your moon.

You and I—
Just you and I—
Together, doing our best to get by within life's insanity.

But who knows how we will end?
When the world is on the edge and often too short.
One thing is for certain: We will both make our mark.
Together we are strong, and apart we are weak.
Try as they may to separate the *you* from the *I*,
It cannot be done because together, we are one.

You Got to Be Good (Song)

When you are feeling down and out.
You feel like you don't have a friend.
All you got to do is just be good.

You got to be good.
You got to be good.
All you got to do is just be good.

When you're feeling sad and lonely.
When you are feeling like you do not have a chance at life.
All you got to do is just be good.

You got to be good.
You got to be good.
All you got to do is just be good.

Jesus is the answer.
He is the only way.
He can sustain you from all your worries.
And sets them all aside.

You got to be good.
You got to be good.
All you got to do is just be good.

Jesus has all the answers.
When you seek him every day?

He will always help you find a way.

You got to be good.
You got to be good.
All you got to do is just be good.

Jesus will help you resist temptations.
He will be your true friend.
He knows your every problem.
If you seek him daily till the end.

He will help you find the way.
You got to be good.
You got to be good.
All you got to do is just be good.

Because all you got to do is just be good.
All you got to do is just be good.
All you got to do is just be good.
So why is there any excuse when all you got to do is just be good?

To Get Away

A place to hide, a place to rest.
A place to get away.
Even if it is for just a day.

Somewhere you do not know.
Somewhere you're not the show.
People talk good about this or that. But they never help you out.
Especially when they think you have no clout.

For me, it does not really matter if things go my way and I get to
get away.
To see unfamiliar things.
To cast a sail toward unfamiliar shores.
To find the life beyond our own back door.
An adventure that is beyond compare.
With so much quiet, you can hear it.

Where people do not brag about a lot of nothing.
For mischief is everywhere; it taints the daily good.
But it will soon go away when I find my little getaway.

To get away, for me, it's just no use.
Even if I want to find my own secret, great escape.
There is always still stuff yet to do.

Alas, I will hang it all up and make my secret, great escape.
To a place no one knows but me.
Within my own place, I do get away.

For in this place, I could write for days without even stopping.
Put my mind to work just like a nonstop clock.
With my words of rhyme.
Could I find someone to appreciate them?
Well, now that is a question.
If not, then they'll just be mine.

Well, however it goes, it will be solitaire at best.
For time can only tell and see if my getaway place even passes the test.
For it to work, I mustn't be disturbed.
I can slumber for as long as I like.
Eat when I'm hungry.
Then work when I want to.

Now, I must go for my voyage is amiss . . .
To find a little get away.
Off, to some tropical paradise that might even be a float.
But I shan't tell it exactly—even in these words that I wrote.

Where Could Your Love Have Went from Me?

Yes, I have been thinking for quite some time and trying to determine within my mind.
Where could your love have went from me?
Did it happen all of a sudden, or did it take a while?
Is it something that crept up on you one night, or did it take several?
Perhaps it took years for you to even discover you were no longer mine or that you neglected my time.

In case you did not know, I've been thinking it over, trying to determine the cause of what went wrong.
Still, yet, I still do not have any answers.
So I am asking you, where could your love have went from me?

My mind wonders and tries to tell me it is just my imagination.
Yet, I know it is not something I am wondering about.
It is a daily chore to seem content.
When I am, but not really.
You see, I know within my very soul that your love is gone.
The only thing to capture is, where could your love have went from me?

Often I lie awake at night, wondering, "Where could your love have went from me?"
The answer has not shown up in my mind.
It just seems to have taken a plunge.

Only a heart racing with discouragement forever present here.
Oh, how I only continue to only ask the question, which is . . .
Where could your love have went from me?

Whirls and twirls within my mind—suddenly baffled by what has become a chronic concern.
Yet, it is very personal, you know, and no one else can ever know except for you and me.
The question remains still: Where could your love have went from me?

We Go the Distance

They call it "distance learning" because we teach while at home.
Yet, we go the distance.
They call our students "special needs."
We call them "exceptional" and "extraordinary" and "able to succeed."
Then, without complaint, we go the distance.

They laugh and criticize us frequently—like our methods lack a plan.
Yet, we work hard every day because, you see, we go the distance.
Do we do our work for a lot of pay?
No, we do not because, you see, we just go the distance.

They often make decisions for us without even asking.
What do we do? We go the distance.
Our students learn every day. "Why?" you may say.
Well, it is amazingly simple: We go the distance.

They laugh and joke about our field—like we don't measure up.
"Why?" you ask. Because we are special educators.
Yet, what do we really do?
Well, it is amazingly simple and clever, you see.
So here it is: We go the distance.

Who's That Gorgeous Girl? (Song)

She looked at an ole picture and asked me a question.
What did she say?
"Who's that gorgeous girl?"
"Who's that gorgeous girl?"
"Who's that gorgeous girl in the whole wide world?"
Then she responded, and this is what she said:
"I'm that gorgeous girl."
"I'm that gorgeous girl."
"I'm that gorgeous girl in the whole wide world."
After a while, I did agree.
"Yes, you're that gorgeous girl."
"You're that gorgeous girl."
"You're that gorgeous girl in the whole wide world."
Once in a lifetime, you'll find one like her.
Then you'll question if it's possible.
To keep a gorgeous girl.
To keep a gorgeous girl.
To keep a gorgeous girl of your very own.
Once you've found her, you'll ask it again.
"Who's that gorgeous girl?"
"Who's that gorgeous girl?"
"Who's that gorgeous girl in the whole wide world?"
Once you have found her, you'll never let her go.
She is the best you'll ever, ever know.

After a while, you'll question it again.
She'll only bring you back to say . . .
"Who's that gorgeous girl?"
"Who's that gorgeous girl?"
"Who's that gorgeous girl in the whole wide world?"

Babies of Mine

Those babies of mine.
First, I waited for you a long time.
Once I saw you, I knew I was so blessed.
All it took was to see your brown curly hair and eyes.
We had a time with our snow cone–drink surprise and your promise to me.
I smiled gently, quite amazed by your confidence.
As we parted, you stole our first kiss.
My heart was taken aback.
I couldn't believe how sure you were.

A long romance has now been going on to raise a son.
Once you came, I watched you grow and gave you all my time.
Then you blessed me with a daughter like you.

She has eyes of blue with a smile that melts your heart.
Her brown curly hair dangles with such, light as it shines.
She is determined to get her way at best.
Those babies of mine.

Now, I know another is soon to be here.
I imagine and hope for one with green eyes like mine.
Who will no doubt stop the show?
A boy who is as strong as an ox, you know.
A fine young man, he will grow up to be.
Just like my first baby, who shares my life with me.

Breakfast for Dinner

Breakfast for dinner—what a time to celebrate!
Some may refuse breakfast for dinner.
Yet, the wise know a blessing in disguise.

We could have eggs, waffles, or pancakes.
Many choices we cannot mistake.
Bring some salsa to go with it.
Even some honey, syrup, or jam.

All make a great meal for one, you can be sure.
Some hot biscuits to entice your evening meal.
Whatever can make you smile, like breakfast for dinner.

Some may not know exactly what it entails for breakfast for dinner.
Their thinking is poor and unaware.
For they do not know of what comes with breakfast for dinner.

Be aware it is not only the food but the company at best.
For no breakfast for dinner comes without a nice guest.
Keep that in mind when you plan for your next breakfast for dinner.

Crooked Ponytails

You are so beautiful with your crooked ponytails.
All dressed up, ready to steal the show.
You love to run, laugh, and play hide-and-seek.
You love to hide under soft and fluffy pillows.
Mostly, you love to be outside—that's for sure.
Taking in the sunshine that lights up your face, smile, and crooked ponytails.
You have grown so fast.
I don't see you much, but my devotion is in my sonnets and in my heart.
Oh, how I adore you with your crooked ponytails and love to see your hair flip and flop as you run away, laughing.
One day, you will meet a gent who will sweep you off your feet.
By then, your crooked ponytails will have gone astray.
But your lovely locks of brown, red, and blond will remain.
Your eyes of blue will charm the hearts of many.
But only one gent will take your heart.
I just hope he is real smart and kind with such an enchanted princess like you.
Knowing that no one else will ever do or even measure up to win my once- little one known as Crooked Ponytails.

Full Moon, What Are You Thinking Of?

Full moon, what are you thinking of?
Are you aware of my sadness tonight?
Does it send you a fright or just brighten your light?
Full moon, what are you thinking of?
Can you show me your light or warm me this night?
I really need the warmth of you or to sit down for a chat or two.

Full moon, what are you thinking of?
Can you give me a hint or distract me a bit?
You are such a great majesty.
Can you shine a little more for me?
You see, you're all I have who can keep me company.

Full moon, what are you thinking of?
Can you solve a problem or two?
I really wish you could be so kind.
Like a true friend of mine.
Tell me your secrets, and I'll tell you mine.

Full moon, what are you thinking of?
I know you're not here to stay and you will soon fade away.
Yet, I know you'll be back to warm the night once more with your
brilliance and delight.
If only you could solve a problem or two.

If only you could return one of my simple pleasures in life with your glistening light.

Full moon, oh, how can it be that you know more than me?
You are a fine one, for sure, and continue to return in your phases at night.
If only you could lend me a hand and take away my loss to let me be young once again with full delight.

How to Impact the World?

How to impact the world?
Many questions we often ask from time to time.
Yet, the one I like best is "How to impact the world?"
We all have a day and a time and need to make our mark.

How to impact the world?
Is it to become extraordinarily rich and flaunt it around?
This cannot be so.
Is it to travel all about and take in all of Earth's delights?
This cannot be so.
Is it to brag about and be a show-off?
This cannot be so.

How to impact the world? Well, let's venture out.
We impact the world when we have no doubt.
When we do for others even without any clout.
We take an unselfish view and care a little more.
That, you see, is quite simple to do.
All you need to do is remember to say "Please" and "Thank you."

In Here and Out There

What you need to succeed is in here.
You try to fight it because you want to be out there.
Yet, you're not ready for out there because you still haven't finished what needs to be done in here.

To be successful, you must be patient and study hard in here.
That way, you'll be ready for out there.
Soon you'll be out there and want to be back in here.
Once you leave, it is more difficult to come back in here.

For your fight is now out there.
Educate yourself and learn so you become wise with your time in here.
To make sure you don't fall short out there.
Now, you are out there but missing the skills needed from in here.

It takes time to learn much from in here.
That way, you are prepared for out there.
After all, you must crawl in here before you can walk out there.
Be sure you're ready in here so things work out fine out there.
Then you know you will do well out there because you were patient enough to learn well from in here.

Love Is Gone

Love is gone, and it has went astray.
No matter what, it can't find its way.
Lost in time without a home or a place to stay.

Words are just meaningless when love is gone.
Good and *kind* can be found when *love* is not around.
You can live with other cares, but love is rarely there.

When love is gone, it is hard to get it back.
It is like a constant fog you're in that can make it hard to see.
You may find yourself in a battle, always trying to bring love back.
Only to find love is gone and good and kind take its place.

When love is gone, you find yourself in a difficult storm.
Like the winds that rage on your tiny ship.
You think your ship will go under, but the stormy winds just carry you on.

Why do you keep up the nonsense to fight it when love is gone?
Well, it is quite simple: You hope for its return.
You would rather fight the storm you're in—
Spinning around as if in a whirlwind—
Than give up and settle for when love is gone.

Perhaps you may find a possibility of your love returning.
Like a little bud blooming in spring.
Even a slight ray of sunshine on a cold winter day.

The bleak rainbow that arrives after the storm.
So why not continue with good and kind?
For a meek sight of hope that love returns.

My Love, My Love, Where Are You?

My love, my love, where are you?
Your love has gone astray and left me here in dismay.
How can it be? For some time, you only loved me.
Then your eyes of dark brown began to let me down.
You looked for someone younger and fairer.

Not wondering if they even care.
You're all about the prize even if it is a compromise.
To keep those eyes from wandering was such a chore.
For so long did I try to do this for.

After a while, why bother so much?
Especially if this cause is lost—
So lost in the deepest pit of desolation.
Perhaps, one day, my love—my love will return.

For now, all I can do is wait within my imagination.
Yet, my hopes grow dim and weary, waiting for a sign you will return
to be near me.
So many times I think to give up.
Knowing that I am only stuck with a tale that has left me far from luck.

If only I could renew myself so you would know me more.
But then, I think, "Whatever for?"

If many years pass by and you don't love me.
Then what will become of me?

Finally, it is certain my courage will give a final tale to my life left uncertain.
We laugh and talk, but that is all.
My love, my love, where are you?

In some mysterious void, I feel.
So far, the eyes cannot even see.
As if I have fallen into an empty pit.
With no hope of finding my way out.

My life is stricken with dread each day.
Without my love—my love—here with me in a sweet serenity.

If only your favor and fondness could return to be my very own.
To no longer ask you with the question of "My love, my love, where are you?"

You may have passed the speed of sound.
In a depth that is beyond any destination.

Search if you must, but you can't be found anywhere—near or far.
For I am left with this final fear, wondering what will bring you near to me.
Time still tells yet, me for you I wait.
With that, I do not hesitate.

Yet still wondering what might be at stake.
Is there really any fate?
Should I continue to contemplate?
Still asking the question, "My love, my love, where are you?"

Oh, Mother of Mine

Oh, mother of mine, how we used to be so close, but you have strayed away.
Whenever I want you near, you make excuses not to be here.
I do my best to honor you, but it is difficult to do.
My life has become a chore to you, and I'm like a distant friend that you rarely see.
My only hope is one day, you'll come back to me.
Oh, mother of mine.

Oh, mother of mine, your mind is still sharp, and age has not let you down.
Yet when I'm with you, in time, you begin to make me frown.
My presence is not your hope or friend, for brothers are your pride and joy.
They have you right in the palm of their hand.

Oh, mother of mine, if you only knew how much I could do for you.
Yet, you tie yourself down to never leave your nest.
Your excuses are no surprise to me because my life is distant and far from yours.

Oh, mother of mine, if you only knew how much I love and care for you.
My prayers are sent up to heaven for you so—far past the clouds.
Oh, how my sadness aches for us and hopes you'll turn around.
To see the daughter who was once a spectacular girl who you often gave the crown.
Oh, mother of mine, so, for now, I just wait to see if you come around.

Oh, mother of mine, you let me play the role of an actress without a real shot.

For I know I have lost the plot.

Yet, every day, I wait for the chance to shine with my shattered crown.

Then try to figure out how it broke apart.

For now, my thoughts have become a shallow heart.

Without a real sense of care to spend much time with you because your mind has gone astray.

Without me in mind or somewhere.

Never keeping me in mind or giving me even a sense of time.

Who will care for you before you make it to heaven's door?

I know this will be my burden to carry because excuses never run dry in my once-lived home.

Where the sons do shine without caring best for you and often leaving you alone.

One day, your Maker will take you home.

Then the duty will be mine again even if in these last years, I never got your time.

Oh, mother of mine, how I lament to have you back before you finally go away.

Off to your Maker's home, and I am left here alone without the joy of your presence today.

Oh, Sir Your Rudeness

Oh, Sir Your Rudeness, how are you today?
It's been a while since you've shown up here.
I almost thought you would disappear.
Yet back again, here you are!

Showing up with a smack that I seem to recall.
Oh, Sir Your Rudeness, how I admire you.
You keep me alert and contrite with you. I feel a challenge when I deal
with you, but you will never know it.

Oh, Sir Your Rudeness, you say things that are supposed to upset me,
but this is not the case.
In fact, I often enjoy this cat-and-mouse chase.
Oh, Sir Your Rudeness, after so many times, I know what to expect,
but it may be too lewd to put it in this text.

So I will just let you know you did not win this game.
Oh, Sir Your Rudeness, sorry—you can't claim any of this fame.
For I won't let you into my heart or brain to tame my soul with your
wicked little game.

One-Sock Girl

One-sock girl, how you're a sight to see.
You make me so happy when you're around.
Oh, how can it be? You remind me of me.

You walk around, looking into this and that.
You don't even care if you have one sock on your foot.
You can light up a room with your one sock on and curls that often hang down in your face. Your smile is ever so impossible to replace.
Yet, you get into trouble and love a good chase.
Then you run with your one sock on.

Right now, I can catch up to you, but I know you'll soon win the race.
All it takes is one look into your face.
That smile won't let you go—not even for a minute, you know.

To tell you the truth, one day, you'll learn.
You only got one sock on.
But for now, I'll write about you and remember the day.
That my one-sock girl who often ran away to play.

Make no mistake as she mesmerizes you.
She will show you some fuss with her one sock on.
So be patient with her and let her grow because one day, she will be a lady.
Who will no doubt steal the show.

Probably Not for Me

We look on the fads and join the crowd but never reflect, "Probably not for me."
Life is simple when we use others' ideas.
Yet, we seldom recollect, "Probably not for me."

For t seems easy to follow the crowd.
Consuming what everyone else does.
Without the inclination, "Probably not for me."

How many times do you buy this or that without a real cause?
Well, think to yourself, "It is probably not for me."
Nothing can help you except your own mind.

Don't let the purchase deceive you.
For you can decide.
For instance, ask yourself, "Do I really need it?"
"How will it benefit me? Is the price worth the purchase?"
Then, once you put it all together, you may suffice that it is probably not for me.

Some Things I Do or Say, Oh Lord (Song)

Some things I do or say, just tend to get in the way,
Oh Lord, oh my Lord.
Some things I do or say, keep me from your goodness all day,
Oh Lord, oh my Lord.

Some things I do or say, aren't my best effort for your highway,
Oh Lord, oh my Lord.
Yet, some things I do or say, let me know I'm forgiven anyway,
Oh Lord, oh my Lord.

Some things I do or say, have me ashamed to be all alone,
Oh Lord, oh my Lord.
Some things I do or say, make me not seek you every day,
Oh Lord, oh my Lord.

Some things I do or say, gotta get outta my way,
Oh Lord, oh my Lord.
Yet, some things I do or say, let me know I'm not alone and I'll
find my way,
Oh Lord—oh, oh, ah, my Lord.

Oh my Lord, I know you're still on the throne today.
Nothing can get in your way.
I will fight that Satan every day.

So I can get to the throne one day—yes!
Oh Lord—oh, oh, ah, my Lord.

One thing I know for sure.
One day, you're coming back to take me home.
Oh, my, my Lord.

Yes, you are, oh, my, my Lord.
Yes—yes, you are.
For sure, you're coming.
To take me home with you one glorious day.
Oh yes, my Lord. On that—that glorious day.
That glorious day.
That glorious day.

Things to Me but Not to You

Things to me but not to you.
Many things to me but not to you cause a fuss with no conclusion.
You are quite the person I want you to be.
But things to me and not to you always get in the way.

Things to me but not to you.
Our conversations often run cold and out of sorts.
With things to me but not to you.

You seem so confused when I disagree.
You're left wondering why things to me but not to you.
If only you could venture out from things to me but not to you.

I remember many laughs you gave me.
When things to me were connected to things to you.
Yes, those were the times when we could combine.
Things to me and to you.
Those were quite-simple days.
When things to me were the same as things to you.

Wondering now, if possible, we could return once more.
Where things to me become the same as things to you.
Yet, I am now frightened they may never return.
Because you're off and gone.
Learning more about things to you but not to me.

To and Fro

To and fro and off we go.
Could it be that Newton knew best?
With his three laws of motion, he did suggest.
Yet, motion does not happen without a force.
It cannot be conquered when the mind and body give in.

To and fro and off we go.
Running in circles, taking in life's pace.
Such a massive rat race.
Don't you know?

To and fro and off we go.
Time is not on our side; it doesn't stop or give a free ride.
Don't take it for granted—this to and fro.
Because it slows with age or without warning.
Don't you know?

Blue Is My New Color

Of the many colors to be fond of mine is simply blue.
Not exactly sure how it became my color.
If you look at my heart, it would show you blue.

"What shade of blue?" you may ask.
Well, that depends on the mood.
Yet, it is always blue.

Of all the shades of blue—well, it really doesn't matter; it is still simply blue.
At times, my blue is as light as a summer day.
With a warmth that touches your skin.
This is the kind of blue I like best. It can be as light as new flowers budding in springtime.

Now, just imagine a cold winter day.
Then you know a new shade of mine.
Picture for yourself being outside and lost in the blistering cold.
Find for yourself the cold wind piercing through your skin.
Then your imagination will take you to my new shade of blue.

Once you're there, you'll know you found me understand this shade of blue because your so, nearby.
Yet, I warn you with all this despair.
Don't pity me or ask too many questions.
"Oh. Why?" you may ask.

Well, that is easy, you see.
You might strike up a new blue within me.
So it is best to let me be.

For I need to contain these new blue shades on my own.
So no one else will ever see except for you and me.

Blue!

Come Run, Come Run

Come run, high in the mountains.
Come run, quick upon the hill.
Come run, your fingers through my hair but only if you dare.

Come run, till you're out of breath.
Only then will you know true success.
Come run, till you're tired and weary and feel about to faint.
Come run, in a secret garden where there are only two.

Come run, to a place no one knows so you feel almost all alone.
"Come run!" will be our chant if it means we become each other's alibi.
Come run, till your heart feels like it may burst and all you feel is a dry thirst.

Come run into a sweet collide.
Come run until you swell up with such a sweet pride.
Wait! Keep on the run because without this chase.
Life is no fun without a race.

Come run, come run, and you can do what you like.
For this run will leave you without a trace of spite.

Forget It

We try to talk, but it is silent.
It is a time for me to say "Forget it."
"Why burden yourself with my ideas? Just forget it."
"I really don't have anything worth sharing with you, so why don't you just forget it?"

"My brain has many ideas, but yours doesn't keep my concern."
"Once again, just forget it."
"You're so fixed on your frame of mind and less on what I have to say."
"So as usual, just forget it."

"Why go into a big conversation when you are not really here?"
"You have too many concerns, but none belong to me."
"Once again, just forget it."

How can I go on with "Just forget it"?
Well, I tell you it is better to forget it rather than fuss over what is important to me.
After all, you have come so close to understanding "Just forget it."
Arguments do not flow over "Just forget it."

We get along with "Just forget it."
Does that mean there is happiness between us?
Well, no—it merely means "Just forget it."
The conversation is stopped with "Just forget it."
Never to be discussed again or talked about.

So easy, isn't it? To just forget it?
Well, don't pity me because I'm used to it, you see.
A conversation would be nice, but it cannot be.
"Why?" you may ask.

Well, it is quite simple.
It is so much easier to quit the strife and use my only device.
Which is "Just forget it."

Good Times before the Wars

Sometimes your finest hours are your good times before the wars.
If you take some time to relax your mind,
Then you'll find those good times before wars.

Planning a strategy may seem like a tragedy, but often it is the good times before wars.
It takes some creating to fight the anticipation of a battle yet to come.
So try to remember our good times before wars.
You may have a laugh with a battle buddy or two, but they are simply good times before wars.
Many will fall, and a lot tend to die.

So try to recognize those good times before wars.
Don't give me any credit because I'm still fighting in it.
Day after day, a battle rages on in my mind, body, and soul.
So all I'm left with is my good times before the wars—unless there really is no good time but only war.

If I Lived By

If I lived by a river, would peace flow by?
If I lived by a mountain, could I touch the sky?
If I lived by a vineyard, would wine flow forever?
So many questions without answers.

If I lived by a glacier, would I have enough ice?
If I lived by a zoo, would I hear many sounds?
If I lived by an amusement park, would I enjoy all the rides?
So many questions without answers.

If I lived by a trail, would I walk every day?
If I could get close to heaven, would you show me the way?
So many questions without answers.
Perhaps you're tired just like me and only expect what comes casually.

Yet, the questions remain. What if I lived by
A river, a mountain, a vineyard, a glacier, a zoo, an amusement park, a
trail, or heaven?
Well, you take your pick to give you a quick and easy fix.
Yet the most precious place is heaven, for that is the place to live.

Leaves of the Fall

Winter, spring, summer, and fall.
Nothing really changes at all.
The work we do is day in and day out.
But we never seem to have enough to shout about.

I never used to want for much.
I was satisfied to have one touch.
But like the leaves of the fall.
It really doesn't matter at all.

We fell in love with just one look.
That is really all it ever took.
We were like the beauty of the leaves of the fall.

Until after they crinkle and after they fall.
And then we don't give much thought to them at all.
Until we work to clean a mess.
That was once a beautiful, lovely place to rest.

Maybe I don't know?

Maybe I don't know?
Maybe I don't know what happens?
It's hard to tell if you really don't know.

You can only guess on life's adventures.
You can only specialize your mind to be ready for the time.

Difficult as it may seem, you can pinpoint a certain scheme.
Don't be disparaged by those dos and don'ts.
Your mind only knows on these issues at best.

Why should you or I be afraid when we can deal the cards all so well?
When you pick the line that fits best?
After all, you know the effects of success.

None will say we are sad about making a profit.
They know too well it is about those dollar bills.
For the more you seek that profit, the more you fall into life's evils.
Then we cannot see beyond it.

It is just based on what we think, believe, and would say. Yet, for some,
they do not know even what that is.

If we say truth, then we are totally unkind.
For we do not know what lurks beyond those simple untruths.
We know nothing about.

Yet can we discover the truth.
I rationalize not because we often blind ourselves.
With those thoughts we often refuse to uncover.

Nothing Compares to You

You are my son's child, and for sure that is true.
But nothing compares to you.
Your smile brings me joy every time you're around.
Since nothing compares to you.
We live most of our lives wondering, "Why the fuss?"
Yet soon we discover how nothing compares to you.

Many a night, we may fret so much over our own.
We often do not see a future to love.
Once you are here, we relinquish all other thoughts.
To discover nothing compares to you.

Take one look at your picture and all hope is lost.
Everyone gives in, forgetting the cost.
"How can it be?" one may ask.
Well, to explain it plainly, we could prove to test.
Let me exclaim and try to figure out this mess.
"Too late," you say. Well, not so fast.

She, with her golden-brown curls, will chase your heart at best.
Run as you may; it is no use.
Just take one look and you'll soon lose the race.
"Why?" you may ask.
Well, the fact remains.
Nothing compares to you.
Not even seconds of your own great fame.

Your eyes are blue, and your head is donned with golden-brown curls.
Your smile is the best sight to see.
To tell you the entire truth and simply put it right.
Nothing compares to you.

For you have been the best since I can't remember when.
I often chase you, and my fun starts again.
Happy to follow you while you take the lead.
To hear you laugh full of joy.

Once again, I am convinced nothing compares to you.
I am sure—without any doubt—of your ability to gain this prize.
For nothing compares to you.

Oh, My Love, How I Think of You

You are extraordinarily strong. I see just how much every day.
You have always been here.
I have never stopped loving you.
Oh, my love, how I think of you.

You need to stay to grow old with me.
We have had tough times, and more will come.
Together we are strong, and we will not be broken.
Oh, my love, how I think of you.

You gave me a great gift, my love.
A son to be proud of.
He is as strong as you. He does his best.
Oh, my love, how I think of you.

I love you, darling, with all my heart.
I can't be here alone, my love.
I need to follow you, my love.
You have made me so strong, my love.
I could not be who I am without you, my love.
Oh, my love, how I think of you.

My love, my darling, I love you so much.
Please stay with me, and my prayer is our Maker takes us together, my love.

That we live and die until the night takes us together to be no more. Oh, how I think of you, my love.

Ole Rooster

Ole rooster, ole rooster, how you crow in the morning.
Ole rooster, ole rooster, how you're always chasing those hens.
Ole rooster, ole rooster, the most beautiful hen tends to your feathers.
Yet, you always run about, ole rooster, chasing all the hens.

You are never satisfied, ole rooster.
You have the best hen in the flock.
Yet, you chase the rest in the henhouse.
They won't even provide you with any chicks.
Ole rooster, ole rooster, when will you ever learn?
Those other hens are not for you.

The best and prettiest one, you already have.
She dedicates her hen life to you even though you run about.
Trying to make more chicks.
Ole rooster, ole rooster, you are great and wise.
Yet, those hens give you such a run.

When will you ever learn, ole rooster, ole rooster?
Your elegant hen waits for you.
She does not run. She does not stress.
She is mighty and confident because she knows you're just an ole
rooster, ole rooster.

Plenty of Time

If you had plenty of time, what would you do?
Would you read as many books as possible?
Until your eyes got weary?
Would you take long walks and enjoy the cool breeze?
Perhaps walk barefoot on the beach?
Would you write many songs and sing them out loud?
Oh, what to do with plenty of time?

If you had plenty of time, would you find many things to laugh about?
Would you enjoy the beautiful nature this world has to offer?
Would you dream day and night?
Would you enjoy your family and friends by having them all around?
Oh, what to do with plenty of time?

Would you share a smile with someone who is down?
Oh, what to do with plenty of time?

If you had plenty of time, would you give it to others?
Would you plant a garden and watch it grow?
Would you share the knowledge you know?
Would you listen to music at the park?
Oh, what to do with plenty of time?

Well, you can contemplate and wonder what to do.
But it is best to do your finest each day.
While helping others along the way.
Then spend your time doing what you enjoy.

For time is short, you see.
In fact, it is only a myth to have plenty of time to spare.

Someone Else Does Not Replace Someone Else

You're gone—never to be seen or loved again.
You were like the child I never had.
We had so many fun times and some sad ones too.
We were always together; Oh, how you made me laugh.

Now, you've been gone many years.
I have been blessed with someone else.
She is a good gift the Lord has given me.
Yet don't forget: Someone else does not replace someone else.

She has the most beautiful eyes of blue, a warm and funny smile.
She has the most beautiful curls and dangling hair.
She is a good gift the Lord has given me.
Yet don't be fooled: Someone else does not replace someone else.

I remember your big ears and sweet smile.
All you needed was the love you never had.
I wanted to keep you for my own, but it was not allowed, you see.
But know that I often think of you because somebody else does not
replace somebody else.

You had bright brown eyes that could melt anyone's heart.
So sweet was your heart and cute big ears you had.
You were the best part of my life, you see.

Before you were wickedly had you taken from me.
So you see, somebody else does not replace somebody else.

My remorse is deep.
Because of what I could have done right, but you see, I lost this fight.
So be sure you know this is true:
Somebody else does not replace somebody else.

The Boy I Do Not Know

I heard you were a boy—
A young child—and was happy to know it.
Yet you remain the boy I do not know.

I hope you are healthy and full of surprises.
Yet you remain the boy I do not know.

One day, you may like knowing yourself as the boy I do not know.
Yet I know many great things will happen for you even if you are the
boy I do not know.

You should not worry if it is strength you need.
You come from a long line of it.
Our line is smart and strong.
I know you will be the same.

A great wonder in this world, and you will make your mark here as well.
It doesn't worry me none if you are the boy I don't know.
I know I will know you soon enough and you will make me prouder
than proud.

After all, you are my son's child, and that is enough for me.
For he is smart and strong, and the same, you shall be.
There is no doubt in my mind you will do the same as he.
Even if you are the boy I do not know for now.
My confidence is brewing.
It is certain: You will be the best boy ever.

No exclamation is required because, you see, you are one of us.

Even if you are the boy, I don't know.
You will no doubt one day become the man I know so well.

The Last Thing I Did

What if the last thing I did, was hug you tight?
What if the last thing I did, was say, good night?
After all, I have no insight, when my last day will come along.
But it will come day or night of that which, I am certain.

What if the last thing I did, was kiss your goodbye?
What if the last thing I did, was pleasure you with my smile?
How can it be that these thoughts wake me up?
Am I still in love with you?
Oh yes, that is for certain.

Judge me if you will with your gestures to start a fight.
But I've come to realize your mine and always will be.

What if the last thing I did, was toss and turn just thinking of you?
What if the last thing I did, was call out for you?
Oh, my love you know it's true. All these years my love remains.
Until my last breath is near and never again.

You my dear are my only care; but one day I must rest forever.
Not, knowing if it's day or night.
So, together while we remain, we must get it right before we say
good night.

Time Travel

If you could time travel, where would you go?
For me, it would be back before you lost your love for me.
It would be back to the time when you would give me the world.

If you could time travel, where would you go?
For me, it would be back to the day I gave you a son.
It would be back to the time I cuddled him close.

If you could time travel, where would you go?
For me, it would be back to our wedding day, and I would walk slower down the aisle.
I would make sure you danced with me before we said good night.

If you could time travel, where would you go?
For me, it would be back to the day we first met.
To say the things we didn't say that first day.

If you could time travel, where would you go?
For me, it would be the day I got your first kiss.
I would have made it linger on my lips somehow.
Instead of acting so starstruck.

If you could time travel, where would you go?
For me, it's easy—I would live my life over for a second round with you.
Hoping to get it all right before my light goes dim.
Before this time stops and my final travel journeys into the end of life.

Anjelitos yo ha un pregunta?
(Song)

Anjelitos, yo ha un pregunta?
Cuando, de Jesus a viene otra vez?
Anjelitos, a ti conosces todas.
Anjelitos, diga que yo esta sperando por Jesus.

Anjelitos, yo ha un pregunta?
Cuando, Jesus viene si yo va contigo y con el?
Anjelitos, a ti conosces todas.
Anjelitos, diga el senor que yo acceptan a va contigo.

Anjelitos, yo ha un pregunta?
Cuando, de Jesus a viene otra vez?
Anjelitos, todo su conosco.
Anjelitos, diga que yo esta sperando por Jesus.

Anjelitos, yo ha un pregunta?
Cuando, Jesus viene si a yo vayan contigo y con el.
Anjelitos, todo su conosco.

Anjelitos, diga a el senor que yo acceptamos que es el Cristo para mi
todavia y seimpre?
Anjelitos, Anjelitos, yo ha un pregunta?
Anjelitos, Anjelitos, Anjelitos.

I Pray Thee, You'll Know How I Loved Thee

There once was a boy without a home.
He often felt life had left him alone.
Then his kin took him in and tried to manage his anger within.
"Why did she do it?" one might ask.

Well, she had seen many griefs such as this.
The boy was quite a task because he missed his mom, you see.
Yet, all he had was me.
Soon, he called me Mom, and I began to feel it too.

Then his blood began to run cold when he visited his mom.
It made it difficult to get him back to his own peace of mind and happiness.
How I often yearned for this because he deserved so much more.
His mother was blind, you see, and could not see what he could truly be.

Her anger ran deep, and she could not give it a rest.
Now I'm lost so deep in the woods without him forever.
I do come out from time to time with bits of happiness here and there.

Yet, my final prayer is you would know.
I pray thee, you'll know how I loved thee.
Oh, how I hope one day, you'll find a bit of peace of mind.
Even though your mom left you so far behind.

I hope you know how I did love you.

I tried so hard to be a good mom to you.
Our distance has now been many years.
I did shed many tears.

How I fought for you to find your way back to me.
But too many lies had been told, you see.
It did not help because others already had a plan.
They stole you away from me without a care to spare.

Now, I pray thee, you'll know how I loved thee.
For that's all I have and hold when thoughts of you distract my mind.
Searching for that one day you'll return to me all on your own.
Then with my final breath, you'll know: I pray thee, you'll know how
I always loved thee.

Shiver and Shake

It is not cold, but I shiver and shake.
It is because of my mental state.
I don't need a diagnosis.
I know it all too well.

Lurking around my room.
It loves the darkness and the night.
I once was good and funny, you know.
Until I served my country for you.

Now, my sleep is all about with all this shiver and shake.
So much so, it used to keep me awake.
Now, I close my eyes, but my enemy is still close by.

He interrupts my dreams.
He plays on my mind with his nightly schemes.
I am not the evil one like others may think.
It is he who leaves me to shiver and shake.
With my battle buddies in my mind's eye.
Such a shattered place to be. "Why does this happen to me?" you say.
Well, the answer is as plain so let me share.
But it will frighten you when I do the stare.
On a path that leads to nowhere.
Only me alone with my shiver and shake.

For now, though, my friend, I will just shiver and shake.
Until I get called again to serve my Maker in the end.

Alas, I no longer suffer from this shiver and shake.

That nightly keeps me awake.

That interrupts and creeps into my dreams so I, shiver and shake.

Bangles and Beads

Oh, how we love things that glitter.
Oh, how we love things that shine.
A sparkle here and a sparkle there with a lot of dangles.
For many a reason, a girl would love bangles and beads.

They make us more beautiful while we dangle them about.
Tossing and turning around us as we move about.
We put them upon us to glisten and shine.
Those beautiful, gleaming bangles and beads of mine.

Oh, how they make me look and feel more refined.
We use them every day on our fingers, ears, and necks.
Oh, how they adorn us to make us stand out.
How they help us look better with refinement among a crowd.

They make us look more beautiful, and we dedicate to match them
upon every outfit.
They are only adornments of bangles and beads, but we love
them anyway.
We often look more professional with these measures of enhancement.
So how we love them—these bangles and beads and their decoration
divine.
That gives us girls our own special kind of shine.
After all, it's those bangles and beads that allow us to steal each show.

When Anger Boils Over

When anger boils over and goes out of control.
Such rage is all I know.
Try to calm my mind, but it is no use.
When a simple call could have made a truce.

Lies are what I'm told by only the so, so bold.
How wretched you are to steal my joy.
My passion in life left long ago.
Such dread do I now know.

Many may not understand such distress.
The burden is not yours to possess.
For wickedness is all around.
It can surprise with a simple sound.

Such dread I now know.
Thinking, thinking, "Why must my heartbeat so?"
What a terrific trick, your ploy.
To get your way at best.
Tricking here and there.
With such a dare.
You do not care.

Oh, how I hate your wicked, wicked ways.
You pass for the devil in disguise.
Wicked and wretched are your schemes.
So tremendously hated by me, it seems.

Oh, mercy on this hate as it rages so.
Stored up with anger that boils over.
Rage—such rage! Oh, how I despise you.

You would even trick your kin so you may win.
You—oh, you are such a joke, playing your simple tricks.
Small eyes cannot see, but you do not trick me.
For I know your knock on my door.
So ask if you will, but never will I let you in anymore.

Take Off Your Boots and Stay Awhile (Song)

Honey, you've been roaming all over town.
Well, it's time for you to settle down.
So come on in. Sit right there.
Take off your boots and stay awhile.

Take off your boots.
Take off your boots and stay awhile.

Listen and I'll tell you a tale or two.
Honey, you know I need you more.
So go ahead and prop up those tired feet.
Take off your boots and stay awhile.

Take off your boots.
Take off your boots and stay awhile.

Honey, I know I got what you need.
Stay right here and you'll agree.
You can't get this love by roaming around.
Take off your boots and stay awhile.
Take off your boots.
Take off your boots and stay awhile.

Honey, my loving is the best around.

You can't find it up in town.
Stay right here with me.
And I will satisfy your needs.

Take off your boots and stay awhile.
Honey, my kind of loving, you can't resist.
Once you get a little kiss.
Take off your boots, and I'll make you smile.
So take off your boots and stay awhile.

Same As You

It is true I may look different with darker skin tones but I'm the same as you.
Oh, yes, my hair may be blonde, red, brown or black.
Yet, I'm still one body that can't go back.
For in this body is human as the blood in my veins.
Sorry, I don't move with a flip of anyone's rein.

For I'm not a deer, horse or a mule.
It is a fact I'm not a puppet or another one's tool.
I do stand on my two feet same as you can't you tell?
So don't cloud up your mind by dropping it into a deep well.

For, I don't get by with a wing or a feather.
My home has a front door same as you.
For this is my sincere decree.
Just look and we'll both agree.
Same as you that is you and me.

Many transgressions I may have but same as you.
So, don't clog your mind as if you're the world's best pride and joy.
For this will lead you into a feeding frenzy in a pond filled with koi.
Seek for yourself this great big favor.

Stop! Building up strife and telling those fables.
For who gives you the right to hand out a false sense of labels?
Now, let's think this through one more time same as you that is me.

Sometimes You Need Combat Boots

To protect your feet while marching on the hot pavement sometimes you need combat boots. To keep your feet warm and dry sometimes you need combat boots. To walk for miles and miles with a ruck on your back sometimes you need combat boots. To hold an M-16 in a foxhole and fire at an enemy on burst sometimes you need combat boots.

For when you get to basic training there is a reason you get two pair. It is not so you have the latest and coolest fashion designer wear. They call everything they give you basic issue item. But what they don't tell you is how many blisters will be on the soles of your feet or that sometimes you need combat boots.

In the line of duty there are plenty of acronyms to go around. Then you better learn them all or suffer a drill sergeants' frown. You'll know that drill instructor right away because their hat looks better than yours any day.
Listen, careful with a cadence call for they expect you to move through it all.

In those combat boots you see all your work gets done. Don't put up a fuss while donning those socks and boots or in the front leaning rest you'll be. Once, your time is done they'll want you back for one more run. Sign on the line and get this GI one more term. Before you know it, your feet are worn from years on end. For this my friend is what happens when sometimes you need combat boots.

Then once you retire from this horse and pony show. To the civilian side for another go. You'll find sometimes you need combat boots one more time. To push them trucks down the assembly line.

My Lovely Self

Most of the time we don't consider how lovely we really are.
Sure, compliments from others are good and nice.
Yet, it is really oneself we should find we genuinely love.
To love yourself is not to be boastful or proud.

It is simply to look at your own splendor for this is allowed.
Consider it however it fits best.
My lovely self will surely pass this test.

A lovely self does not consider another's approval.
For a lovely self's mind is made up from confidence that comes
from within.
It does not consider the color or criticize its own skin.
It simply looks from what is down deep inside.
Without any amount of pride.

It does not deal with a measure of doubt.
Or listen to others while they spout about.
For my lovely self is far too wise.
It is pure and real without any disguise.

It does not concern itself with another's opinion.
For my lovely self has full dominion.
It does not seek after glory or fame.
For my lovely self that would be oh, so mundane.
So, by knowing all this put on your lovely self every day.
For if you do this all things will surely go your way.

Space and Time

We may argue or fuss with each other.
What if I could solve this dilemma for you?
Would you find that it may be true?
Well, why not give it a chance and try?

What we really need is space and time.
They say time can heal the broken hearted.
Yet, we don't consider the need for space.
To solve a problem, it is true it takes time.

Yet, to grow we all need space.
When trouble occurs why not take your space and time together?
For it is wise, to give space along with time.

Once, you are calm then you can solve things while keeping your
wits about.
For all you need is to give yourself is a little space and time.
Indeed, good things will happen with some space or time.

For ask a friend and I'm sure they will agree.
It takes space and time to save yourself from an enemy.
For if you jump into a bickering mess.
All you pay yourself is much more distress.

So, be oh, so wise to take my advice.
For many years it has taken me.
To learn a more practical way to disagree.

What is it one might ask?
Well, is it to go for miles with your head hung down?
This can't, be it?
When there is a simpler way to avoid a fight.

It begins with a little bit of space and time.
Then many of men have fought in wars for years.
When they could have saved that battle instead.

How do you ask once again?
Well, to be frank it is space and time.
This is the best way one can agree.
Is to allow space and time to regain one's own mind.

Oh, Cast Out Your Paintbrush

Oh, cast out your paintbrush on canvas.
To sketch a landscape or two.
I will share my rhymes with you. While you paint your beautiful landscapes.
Together we can be quite successful with each our own gift.

Oh, cast out your paintbrush to sketch your best masterpiece.
For mine is with words and rhyme you see.
For a long time, we did not agree. Then one day you came back to me.

Oh, cast out your paintbrush because I always knew you had a great gift. Then in time I began to realize mine.
Now, it is time for us to agree.
So, we can become our best you see.
Putting our great gifts together like we planned as children you know?
It is true that was such a long time ago.

Oh, cast out your paintbrush and give it a go.
For it is not too late for us you know.
The time is now do not hesitate.
For your colors can make something especially great.

Oh, cast out your paintbrush to create your own version of paradise.
For your eyes can see natures beauty is out there.
Then put it to canvas you know.

Oh, cast out your paintbrush for this is my pleading sonnet just for you.

To place another landscape on.
Oh, cast out your paintbrush without regret.
For the world has not seen your best one yet.

Pretty and Precious

If you haven't seen her, you've missed quite the mark.
She can move your very heart.
She will enchant you with a twirl or two.
As she rushes through the grass that has a hint of dew.

Fuss over her you may!
Only, to see her laugh and even run away.
Then, she'll melt your heart and lungs, till you can breathe again.
All the while trying to run as if she can outsmart the wind.
Why do you say? It easy to see how pretty and precious she can be.

Falling in love with her is easy of course.
She will not bring any kind of remorse.
Once you gaze upon her then you'll know.
Meanwhile, she's got you on the go.
For so pretty and precious is she.
That every eye can see.